Southern Region Multiple Unit Memories

Littlehampton
Station entrance

Compiled by Adrian Willats

© Images and design: Transport Treasury 2024 Text: Adrian Willats

ISBN 978-1-913893-48-4

First published in 2024 by Transport Treasury Publishing Limited. 16 Highworth Close, High Wycombe, HP13 7PJ.
Totem Publishing an imprint of Transport Treasury Publishing.

www.ttpublishing.co.uk

Printed in Tarxien, Malta by Gutenberg Press Ltd.

'*Southern Region Multiple Unit Memories*' is one of many books on specialist transport subjects published in strictly limited
numbers and produced under the Totem Publishing imprint using material only available at The Transport Treasury.

Front Cover: On a sunny Sunday 30th May 1982, Robert and I had travelled up to London to see the second departure and inaugural arrival of the newly introduced Venice Simplon-Orient-Express. With several hours between the two chances to photograph the magnificently restored Pullman cars, we took some pictures at other stations. Here we see 4EPB 5188 in the through platforms at London Bridge, the large brown structure behind being the enclosed footbridge between platforms installed as part of the station's then most recent 'modernisation'. Headcode 62 indicates a train from Charing Cross to Gillingham via Lewisham and Erith.

Frontispiece: Still in use in 1984 was this station building at Littlehampton. Long time friend and fellow traveller Robert Martin looks on as I take my slide on 4th June during our Area B rover week. It had been planned to provide a new building in the 1930s, but wartime damage intervened and repaired existing facilities had to remain in use until the arrival of Network SouthEast in 1986. Although taken after his tenure as BR Chairman, this image might perhaps remind us of Sir Peter Parker's remarks about "The crumbling edge of quality" and the fun poked at BR's marketing slogans of the time – this was after all, we were told, "the age of the train". Unfortunately, 'age' can be taken in different ways!

Rear Cover: After a stop long enough for passengers to seek refreshment and other 'facilities', (not to mention visiting the onboard SEG sales stand!), the "Sussex Slammer" tour of 19th November 2005 leaves Littlehampton for the next leg of the day's itinerary. Unit 1866 now brings up the rear as the train passes the semaphore signals still controlling train movements at that time. No one appears to have moved the headboard after arrival earlier!

Introduction

The story behind this book begins early in 1978, on a footbridge over the railway between Havant and Bedhampton stations in Hampshire. I was studying for my A Levels at Havant College and one day the usual friend with whom I chatted over our sandwiches at lunchtime was off sick. I went for a walk and started chatting with a fellow student who was watching the trains. His name was Robert Martin, and that day was the beginning of a friendship and shared enjoyment of the transport hobby that has so far lasted some forty-five years.

This, my first book, is intended to be a pictorial record of some of the trains that I have seen, photographed and travelled on during that time. It is not intended to be exhaustive and is a purely personal selection from my colour slides. Most were taken with an Olympus OM10 camera using Agfa CT100 film. During brief periods when Agfa was not available, slide films were bought from Boots and Supasnaps. The pictures show various types of electric and diesel electric multiple unit trains that were operated by the Southern Region of British Rail. I have tried to keep technical detail to a minimum, as some railway knowledge on the part of readers is assumed.

I have not explained Southern Region classification of trains (2EPB, 4VEP etc) as various excellent and detailed reference books are available for those seeking more detail. Particularly useful for numbers and unit formations was "British Railways Electric Multiple Units to 1975" (by Hugh Longworth, published by OPC/Ian Allan in 2015). If I know the exact date of an image, it is given. If not, I have narrowed it down as far as possible.

Any opinions expressed are purely my own and if I am not sure of any details (the oldest slides were after all taken in 1982!) then I have been honest and said so.

My thanks are due to Kevin and Robin at Transport Treasury Publishing for giving me this opportunity and for their kindness, help and encouragement; to Rebekah for turning my 'raw material' into a finished book; to the friends who have in many ways added to the pleasure and enjoyment of the transport hobby; to my wife Wendy for tolerating that hobby over more than thirty years and our daughter Eleanor for not making too much fun of Dad and giving occasional and valuable 'tech' advice!

Most of all though, to the person who has shared this interest with me since that first meeting during that college lunchtime all those years ago. I am sure that looking at these pictures will bring back memories of many of the travels that we have enjoyed together over many years. May there be many more – at least for as long as age and health allow!

Thank you, Robert.

Left: Seen from the enclosed footbridge at Clapham Junction sometime in August 1982, Driving Motor Brake Second S14409S forms one end of 4EPB 5429. Note that the unit is in blue and grey livery and carries its number twice on the yellow end. Numbers were applied in this fashion when units had been internally refurbished, or – to use the term favoured by the Southern Region at that time – 'facelifted'. This involved replacement of 'naked' light bulbs with fluorescent tubes and reupholstering of seats.

Right: On the same day the first of the four-car, sliding door units of Class 508 calls at Clapham Junction on a service to Shepperton. Forty-three of these units entered service between January 1980 and December 1982, the design being derived from the 'PEP' prototypes introduced in 1973. Two four car and one two car PEPs were built and ran in passenger service on various suburban routes on the Southern. Their purpose was to thoroughly test all the new technology fitted before production batches were authorised. The first of these were Class 313 (three car sets) for the Great Northern suburban electrification and later variants included Class 315 for the Great Eastern lines out of Liverpool Street, Class 507 for Merseyside and Class 314 for the Glasgow area. Class 315 were four car sets, the others consisted of three cars.

Left: The last of three slides from that rather grey August 1982 day sees 4CEP 1532 calling at Waterloo East with a Kent coast service. Originally built in 1958-59, (after six prototype units a few years earlier), the first set to be experimentally refurbished, 7153, was so treated in 1975. In 1979, work began to refurbish the rest of the class, although some features of 7153's treatment were not perpetuated. Originally, when outshopped from Swindon after their refurbishment, full six-digit numbers beginning with the TOPS class number (411) were carried. Later examples carried the shorter version, as seen here. Original numbers had been in a series 7101 to 7211 with the 4BEP version (having a buffet car) being units 7001 to 7022. Only seven 4BEPs (Class 412) were refurbished, becoming 2301 to 2307.

Right: On 21st August 1982, better weather was evident as we waited at Fratton for a DEMU to take us on to Southampton. Living on Hayling Island back then, our nearest station was Havant. Until the Solent Link electrification inaugurated in May 1990, any westward trips involved taking an electric train from Havant to Fratton, where a change was necessary to the diesel-electric multiple-units (DEMUs) operating services from Portsmouth Harbour to Southampton and Salisbury. While waiting, I photographed 4CAP electric unit 3308 on a semi-fast Brighton service. These units had been formed by semi-permanently coupling pairs of 2HAP units and renumbering the result. The platform canopies unfortunately throw much shadow when a train occupies platform 1, but the clean cab end is nicely lit – not many dead insects on it yet!

Left: Functional though the cab end design of the 4BEP/4CEP units was, it could scarcely be described as stylish! Some improvement was achieved with the 4BIG and 4CIG units, the first of which (7301) emerged in 1964. Unit 7418 is seen having arrived at Portsmouth Harbour in August 1982, showing the recessed housings for the connecting cables and the softer, rounded join of cab end and roof. On the left, the unit type (4CIG) is in black, with the TOPS class (421) shown by a blue sticker above. Twin horns are mounted on the roof. Two red 'blanks' are wound up in the headcode box as this vehicle will be the rear end of the train on departure.

Right: Seen from an arriving train are three types of EMU in Waterloo's platforms in October 1982. From left to right are 508007, 4SUB 4680 and 4EPB 5110. The 4SUBs were the predecessors of the 4EPBs and were built from 1940 to 1951. The last was withdrawn from service in 1983.

Far Left: Seen at Victoria on 15th October 1982 is motor luggage van (MLV) 68010, numerically the last of ten of these vehicles built in 1959. They were used to provide additional luggage and mail space to that available in the brake vans of the 4BEP and 4CEP units forming boat trains from London to Dover and Folkestone. They had a cab at each end and could work for short distances off the third rail by using battery power. Becoming TOPS Class 419, they later sported 'unit' or 'set' numbers (despite being only a single vehicle!) (41)9001-10.

Near Left: Also seen at Victoria on 15th October 1982 is 4CEP 1531, possibly the other end of the same train as MLV 68010. The unit is in platform 1 and visible above is the painted advertisement for Bishop & Sons that has featured in photographs taken over many years.

Right: On a journey home from London in October 1982 our train called at Horsham, where 4SUB 4680 was stabled in the sidings next to the platforms. A slight impression of 'UFOs' is provided by the reflections of our own train's roof mounted light bulbs!

A 'matching set' of three 4VEP units, uniformly attired in standard blue and grey livery, occupy platforms 2, 3 and 4 during what appears to be a quiet spell at Brighton on 19th March 1983. The first twenty of these units, originally intended for suburban use, were built in 1967. The class eventually totalled 194 four car sets, with the last examples not being built until 1974. All were built at the BR carriage works in York.

Still in use at Brighton on 19th March 1983 was the mechanical train departure board. Antiquated it may perhaps have appeared in the 1980s, but all the information passengers need is clearly visible – train destinations and calling points, any additional notes such as special bus services for part of the journey, (note chalked wording!), platform number required and, in the form of a good old-fashioned analogue clock face, the time of departure! Although this impressive device has of course long since been replaced, one can't help but think of the old adage "If it ain't broke, don't fix it" – but then progress sadly takes no account of such sentiments. However, perhaps a mechanical device might still work without electrical power – a tall order no doubt for its digital, 'flashing light' successors!

A pair of 4VEPs stand in the down platform at Havant on 12th May 1984, probably on a service from Waterloo to Portsmouth Harbour. My modest 135mm telephoto lens picks out the detail along the sides of these units, with their door to every seating bay in the open saloon sections and to one side of each first-class compartment. The short side corridor alongside these compartments is visible on the nearest driving end vehicle, with the corresponding compartment side on the furthest one by the signals. Note that Havant at this time retained both up and down through lines, used by freight, engineering and parcels trains – plus the occasional railtour! When the line was first electrified in 1937, fast trains were not intended to call there, hence the loops serving the two platform faces. Later, however, housing development generated much more commuter traffic and by the time I first used the station for enthusiast travels in 1978, few if any normal passenger services missed out a Havant call.

13

Left: The rear of an eastbound, formed of 4CIG 7326, is seen at Chichester on 12th May 1984. At one time the station had bay platforms on both sides and although that on the other side of the current westbound platform had disappeared by 1984, the other was still there and on this day was occupied by Class 73 electro-diesel loco 73136. Now only the two tracks remain, and road vehicles now encroach much nearer to the platform. The first thirty-six 4CIGs, (including this one), had comfortable deep-cushioned seats with what I liked to call 'nodding wings' on the gangway side of the seat pairs. Seating quality and comfort has, it must be said, varied over the years since Mark 1 stock such as these was in widespread use. I miss their comfort – and I suspect many a reader might agree.

Right: 4CIG Driving Trailer Composite (Lavatory) S76810 leads unit 7389 in a calm scene at Havant in May 1984. The bridge visible carries Park Road North over the tracks and the platform fence (wall?) visible to the left is of the standard concrete type widely seen on the region. The train has a green light to head for Portsmouth, with a red one showing for the through line. The lavatory is at this end, hence the opaque yellow 'window'. A more favourable coincidence of transport modes might have seen a Southdown or Portsmouth Corporation bus crossing the bridge, but clearly such luck of timing was not with me that day!

A May 1984 panorama of Havant station sees 4VEP 7805 heading for either Waterloo, Victoria or Brighton. On the far left, the 'public' footbridge ascends to cross the station (top of picture) and reach both the town centre station approach and the park. This walking route does not give or require entry to the station – the station's 'internal' footbridge being visible just beyond the far end of the train. A third footbridge in the far distance enables pedestrians to cross the line when the level crossing gates are closed to road traffic. All three footbridges (plus the one carrying Park Road!) remain in use at the time of writing in early 2023, the one connecting the platforms having been modernised to provide lift facilities.

A 4VEP unit is seen in Fratton's platform 2 ready to make the final two stops on its journey at Portsmouth & Southsea and Portsmouth Harbour. The four first class compartments are nearest the camera, with the orange curtains as fitted in such accommodation at that time. Fratton station can be extremely busy on football match days, (often requiring heavy police presence), as Portsmouth FC's home ground, Fratton Park, is not far from the station. A few yards further on from the footbridge, the road crosses the tracks by means of Fratton Bridge. Until final withdrawal of Portsmouth's trolleybuses in 1963, this had been one of the most complicated overhead wiring junctions in Great Britain, with several roads converging. The slide was another from May 1984.

17

While doing some general railway photography at Eastleigh in May 1984, my 135mm lens allowed me a slightly closer view of something a little more unusual! 4TC Trailer Corridor First S70848 had suffered fire damage and is seen (it appears to be still formed with the rest of unit 405) awaiting repairs. These unpowered four car sets had been introduced for the electrification to Bournemouth in 1967. A 'push-pull' system was devised, whereby a powered 4REP unit would propel ('push'!) one or two 4TCs from Waterloo to Bournemouth, controlled by the driver in the leading 4TC cab. On arrival, the 4TCs would be uncoupled from the 4REP and a Class 33 diesel-electric loco would couple up to the 4TC(s) and haul them to Weymouth. Departure from Weymouth involved the loco propelling the 4TC stock to Bournemouth where they would be coupled to the rear of a waiting 4REP and the diesel loco detached. The 4REP would then haul the TC stock to Waterloo.

The 4REP units had powerful motors (rated at nearly 3,000hp) as they were required to power up to twelve coaches on the Waterloo-Bournemouth route. They also included a buffet car, these being rebuilt from loco-hauled stock, as were many of the REP and TC vehicles. This May 1984 view shows buffet car S69024 (of unit 3014) at Eastleigh. This was not one of the original 1967 4REPs, but one of an additional four which entered service in 1974 (along with three more 4TCs) when the frequency of Waterloo-Weymouth fast services was increased from two-hourly to hourly. The buffet cars had loose chairs (for twenty-three passengers) at the tables, but as a full restaurant service was provided on many workings, tables were also fitted to seating bays in the adjacent motor coach. Pub sign style 'names' were carried, but only internally at the buffet counters.

A new service introduced in May 1984 was the dedicated "Gatwick Express" specifically to cater for airline passengers and running non-stop from Victoria to Gatwick Airport. No new stock was involved but, as with the earlier Bournemouth scheme, both converted or refurbished stock and a push-pull method would be employed. Mark 2f former loco-hauled coaches were refurbished and converted to form semi-permanent two car (Class 488/2) and three car (Class 488/3) sets. At one end of the coaches, power would be supplied by a Class 73 electro-diesel. At the other, a former 2HAP Motor Brake Second was used, stripped of all its former seating and given a guard's office and large luggage area. Gangway connections were fitted at the non-driving end. The result was classed as GLV (Gatwick Luggage Van) and ten were provided as Class 489.   GLV 9101 is seen leaving Victoria in the first few days of the new service.

GLV 9109 is seen at Gatwick Airport in May 1984. Wrap-around application of the yellow end resulted in the BR double arrow being applied in black, with the rest of the sides being in "Inter-City" livery to match the passenger coaches. At busy times of the year, eight passenger coaches were used – two three car sets and one of two cars. With lighter loading expected in the 'winter' timetable, just one of each type provided five coaches for passenger use.

On 20th November 1983, refurbished 4BEP 2303 is seen at Havant leading a 4CIG on a service to Waterloo. Headcode 82 indicates that the train would serve more stations than the fastest services (81) which, after Havant, only served Petersfield, Haslemere, Guildford, Woking and Waterloo. The slowest services (83) called at everywhere as far as Woking, then only at selected stations onwards to Waterloo.

21

Also on 20th November 1983, unit 2303's buffet car (S69343) is seen at Havant. When these units began running on Portsmouth-Waterloo trains in 1983, my father (who worked for Kenwood at Havant, by then part of the Thorn Group) was making rail journeys with colleagues to visit another Thorn site at Spennymoor in County Durham. The first leg would be by electric train to Waterloo, onwards from Kings Cross being by Inter-City 125 High Speed Trains. One day, obviously having occupied seats in the 4BEP on that day, dad came home and said that they had travelled from Havant on a 'new train'. I had to produce some degree of 'evidence' courtesy of contemporary railway magazines, to convince him otherwise! One slightly retrograde step with these buffet units, at least in the opinion of some of us at the time, was that the previously available toasted sandwiches ceased to be offered. This was due, apparently, to the previous 4BIG buffet cars having had a grill, whereas the refurbished 4BEP buffet cars were instead equipped with a microwave. Progress?...

In 1984 the Southern Region offered four 'rover' tickets (Areas A, B, C & D) which allowed unlimited travel on seven consecutive days within the area specified and using any train. We opted for Area B, with its western boundary being Portsmouth Harbour. Included were all the east and west 'Coastway' lines, with travel inland by certain routes allowable to places such as Horsham, Haywards Heath and Three Bridges. The eastern extremity was at Hastings, with just a short section of the DEMU-operated route being available as far as Battle. The cost for all this was just £12, with the only restriction being that no trains before 0900 on weekdays could be used. As it happened, we only travelled on the Monday to Saturday, (4th-9th June), as we wanted to attend a vintage bus event near home on the Sunday, but we still visited many places for the first time and saw, photographed and travelled on most types of rolling stock in service at that time. In this view taken on 9th June, 4CIG 7438 has arrived at Hastings while DEMU 1013 waits to leave for Charing Cross via Tonbridge. The contrast between the curved, wider body profile of the electric unit with the narrower, straight-sided bodywork on the "Hastings" unit is clearly visible.

DEMU Trailer Composite S60700 is seen at Hastings on 9th June 1984. The diesel units (all of six cars) were introduced in 1957 and were withdrawn in 1986. Three types were built, two with 'long' coaches (63' 5") and one batch with 'short' (56' 11") coaches. The two types of units with the longer coaches were classed as 6L or 6B – the latter having a buffet car. The sets with shorter vehicles were 6S. This vehicle was originally all-first class, but in the spring of 1980 all Hastings unit trailer firsts were altered to composites by the downgrading to second class of two compartments in the longer vehicles or, as in the case of the shorter examples such as S60700, just one – visible on the far right of this view. The individual doors show that this is the non-corridor side.

24

On 9th June 1984, diesel units 1035 and 1036 leave Hastings for Charing Cross. I freely admit that this somewhat 'arty' view was NOT my original idea – I took inspiration from a similar picture that I had seen in a railway magazine. The other photographer had however taken a monochrome image, so by using colour slide film I had at least chosen a different medium in which to try to capture a different style of railway image. The bridge carried a road over the railway and was quite a walk from the station, but I hope that readers will agree that the result was worth the effort! Good weather will be noted in these Hastings views – I should add that we were very lucky over the six days on which we travelled, with only a brief wet interlude on the Thursday afternoon.

Left: On 9th June 1984, the driver climbs down from 3H DEMU 1111 after arrival at Hastings from Ashford. At the time, this was the only one of the 3H sets to have been modernised, with new interior lighting and gangways between coaches within the set. It was variously referred to at the time as 3H(M) or 3H(R) – for 'modernised' or 'refurbished'. Quite why he was climbing down to track level rather than 'alighting' from the other side I wasn't entirely sure at the time! In more recent times, this platform face was reduced in length when station modernisation included a level walking route from the platform to the station exit.

Right: At the time of our Area B travels, we were aware of a diagram whereby a nine-car formation of three car DEMUs worked to Eastbourne on a Tuesday, after which the units were dispersed to their allocated depots. I think that they had worked down from Selhurst depot, presumably after attention there and probably not in passenger service. I apologise for a bit of vagueness here, but I did not keep records of exactly what was involved – suffice it to say that we knew that if we were at Eastbourne for enough of a Tuesday, we would be in with a chance of getting some pictures! Here the formation is seen after arrival at Eastbourne on 5th June 1984. Nearest the camera is 3H 1108, with another 3H (1120) partly visible beyond – both are in blue and grey livery. The third unit, 3D 1309 (nearest the buffers and not visible here) was still in all blue livery.

On 1st September 1984 Robert and I travelled on our first ever railtour, the "508 Twilight" organised jointly by the Southern Electric Group (SEG) and the Locomotive Club of Great Britain (LCGB). The Class 508 units were coming to the end of their few years on the Southern Region and three out of four coaches of each unit were to be transferred to Merseyside, where similar Class 507s already operated as three car units. The vehicles remaining on the Southern would be inserted into new Class 455/7 units, only three coaches of each of which would thus have to be newly built. Unit 508025 is seen with the tour at Shepperton. On the far platform are metal weights, which were used when commissioning new stock to simulate passenger loadings. Note the prominent SEG headboard, (the smaller LCGB one being carried on the other end) and the displaying of 'Special' and 'SEG LCGB' on the destination blinds.

The "LCGB end" of the "508 Twilight" tour is seen during a pause at Waterloo part way through the day's itinerary. As the tour train was formed of just the one unit, rather than repeatedly and pointlessly writing its number on my slide index card, I simply put, for example - "SEG end at Shepperton" or "LCGB end at Waterloo". In those days, one could buy from branches of Boots pairs of 36-slide projection magazines, with an index card on which to write details, all in a plastic box. Those days are long gone!

The "508 Twilight" tour is seen at Guildford. This major station, in a cathedral and university town at the hub of several rail routes, was looking at bit tired at this time, with the platform canopies in need of some attention. Eventually, they were all replaced with new ones, together with new platform buildings and station entrances – but this was still some years in the future as tour passengers and others are seen, each trying to get their own photos of the occasion.

An 'elevated' view of the "508 Twilight" tour ("LCGB end") from the footbridge at Virginia Water. Note that at this end there was no special lettering in the destination displays – 'Special' merely being shown twice. Much interest was shown in the tour, with a good load of passengers having booked tickets. This was despite the stock involved being modern and only a few years old, which goes to prove I suppose that railway interest is not all about nostalgia and the past!

Two 'Special' blinds have returned to the "SEG end"! As we take our leave of 508025 at the end of the tour, the unit keeps company with 4VEP 7734 at Waterloo. On the platform beyond the 4VEP can be seen a couple of yellow passenger luggage trolleys and what looks like part of a blue 'BRUTE' – I believe the letters were supposed to stand for "British Rail Universal Trolley Equipment" and at one time they could be seen everywhere, often piled high with parcels and sacks of mail. The yellow trolleys had the wording "Not to be removed from…", followed by the name of the 'owning' station. No doubt this was to discourage them from 'wandering' elsewhere, although I seem to remember on a holiday in 1993 seeing one at Blackpool North (or somewhere thereabouts) marked "Not to be removed from Portsmouth Harbour"!

When 4SUB unit 4732 was the last of the class to receive a repaint, (at Selhurst in 1982), it was turned out in a mock-Southern Railway green livery, with mostly yellow cab ends but including a green section at the top. On the green area was the word "SOUTHERN" in 'sunshine' type shaded capitals, with the unit number in similarly shaded numerals underneath. After the last of the 4SUBs were withdrawn in 1983, 4732 was retained for charter and special train use. For a few years afterwards, it often operated on such workings coupled to the two car 2BIL unit 2090, which had been saved for the National collection upon withdrawal in 1971. By 1984, 2090 had been restored to main line running standards and we joined it and 4732 on the "Electric Phoenix" tour, starting and finishing at Brighton, on 23rd September of that year. Here the tour is seen during a lunchtime stop at Waterloo. This was again a joint SEG/LCGB affair, but in lieu of the usual small LCGB headboard on the 2BIL, there was a larger one mentioning also the involvement of the National Railway Museum as owners of the unit. Unfortunately, the headboard included the mis-spelt word 'Pheonix'… Once again, BRUTEs are on the platform and, to prove that even in the 1980s railtour clientele wasn't exclusively male, a young lady is alighting from the tour train!

An enthusiast at Waterloo watches me photographing Class 455/7 unit 5703 during the Waterloo lunch stop of the "Electric Phoenix" tour. This, it may be recalled, was one of the batch of 455s that received ex-Class 508 trailers – the second vehicle, just visible on the right, is one of them; its lower, flatter roof profile contrasting with that of the driving trailer. In the 1980s, despite some possible danger from IRA terrorism, the man was probably not as likely as he might be now to be accosted by some 'jobsworth' running up to him and shouting at him not to leave his bag lying around. Passengers have for a long time, first by poster and nowadays by seemingly endless announcements, been urged not leave items unattended – and for perfectly sensible reasons. I still remember, in those now far off 1980s, seeing such a poster inside a London Underground tube carriage. Showing simply a picture of a large suitcase, it featured the words "If you see an unattended bag…" Some wit had written underneath "Go up and talk to her!"

Left: One of the 'extremities' of the electrified network visited by the "Electric Phoenix" was Ore, a short distance east of Hastings. Here two passengers converse with the driver before the train retraced its steps back towards Hastings. I thought I had a vague memory of entering this slide in a Hayling Camera Club competition, but if I did it must have been before I started keeping my own records of how well (or otherwise) my entries scored. Or perhaps memory is just playing tricks?...

Right: One of the afternoon photo stops of the "Electric Phoenix" was at Portsmouth Harbour, where earlier dull weather had given way to some quite pleasant sunshine. Here the door handles of 'three and a bit' coaches of 4732 are picked out against its "Southern" green as the tour train stands in platform 2.

More 'sunlit SUB sides' (as I wrote on my slide box index card! Part of 2090 gets in on the act on the left and the two slides showing this effect are a reminder that in the days before cameras were 'auto-everything', you had to set either exposure (lens aperture) or shutter speed carefully to achieve the desired result. In my case, with the Olympus OM10, it was the aperture that I had to choose, the camera then selecting the shutter speed. In addition, slide film had a much narrower margin for errors of exposure than print film, requiring even more care in one's choice of settings.

During the Portsmouth Harbour stop of the "Electric Phoenix", a comparison of unit ends shows S12123S of 2BIL 2090 and 12795 of 4SUB 4732 – a Driving Trailer Composite (Lavatory) and Driving Motor Brake Second Open. The coaches – and indeed whole units – dated from 1937 and 1951 respectively. With the abolition of three classes of rail travel in Britain in the first half of the twentieth century, original second class was dispensed with, leaving only first and third provided. The increasing absurdity of this was eventually officially realised with third being redesignated as second in 1956. In more recent times, 'second' has been in turn redesignated as 'standard', along with 'passengers' becoming 'customers'.

Not wishing to carry a tripod on railtours, (although at that time I did possess one), a steady hand and/or perhaps a handy platform trolley to rest the camera on might hopefully give a fair result in cases such as this. The 2BIL is seen at Brighton at the end of the "Electric Phoenix" tour. A most enjoyable day, during which each passenger had been allocated a 'leg' of the itinerary during which they were allowed seat in the 2BIL, to ensure that everyone got a chance to ride in the older unit! Behind is Motor Brake Second Open S62069, then formed in 4BIG unit 7047.

One aspect of the British Rail era always popular with enthusiasts who remember those years was the open day – giving a rare chance for the public to visit railway depots or workshops. I certainly remember attending several on the Southern Region – for example, those at Eastleigh, Wimbledon, Bournemouth, Ashford and Brighton. These would be major events at large sites, with both local and visiting motive power on display, together with traders' stalls selling all manner of items to help empty visiting enthusiasts' wallets! One of the more unusual open days that we attended in those days was held in 1984 at the very small workshops at Ryde, on the Isle of Wight. Even more out of the ordinary was the time of year chosen – the end of January! Converted London Underground tube stock had been in use since early 1967 on the only remaining part of the BR network on the island – the eight and a half miles from Ryde Pier Head to Shanklin. The earliest tube cars used were built in the 1920s and one vehicle, trailer S43, would reach its sixtieth birthday in 1984. Celebratory logos were carried on the outside, with '1924' and '1984' either side of the BR double arrow logo. Special framed photographic displays were mounted inside the car. Early grey weather improved later to give this rather pleasant sunset scene at Shanklin. The sun, perhaps unexpected that day, did cause a problem with the slide shows, as it was not possible to 'black out' a railway workshop for projection purposes!

One of the coastal termini that we visited during our Area B week was Littlehampton. Here we see 4CIG 7326 in platform 1 on 4th June 1984. Not only is there much lineside 'growth' visible on the left, but weeds are also beginning to come up between the running rails. Although visits by the weedkiller train may have been more frequent back then than they appear to be nowadays, they can't be everywhere all the time – and weeds, as we know from our own gardens, don't need long to get established! A wooden item vaguely resembling a cricket bat will be noted in the left hand cab window. This was used, I am told, as an insulator should it be necessary to lift current collection shoes on electric stock.

Two units are seen at the buffers at Littlehampton on 4th June 1984. Nearest the camera is 4CIG 7320, with 4VEP 7783 beyond. Although it is now some years since the last of these Mark 1 units were finally withdrawn from service, selecting slides and writing these notes to accompany them instantly takes me back to those early years of our rail travels. These trains, together with older HAP and EPB stock and the DEMUs, took us to places all over the Southern Region. Admittedly, by 1984 we did have some Class 455s on the region and, (though not for much longer) Class 508s too, but most trains that passengers used on the Southern were derived from BR Mark 1 coach designs or their Southern Railway predecessors. It is always easy to think that what is in service 'now' will always be there, and I realised years later that I perhaps should have taken more pictures than I did of the everyday rail scene. Another life lesson learned!

This is our penultimate train of the day on 4th June 1984, seen at Barnham where we changed trains for Havant. The rear unit on this service from London is 4TEP 2702, one of four temporary buffet units formed from three coaches of a refurbished 4CEP with an unrebuilt 4BEP buffet car not required for the refurbishment programme. This was to provide cover for buffet cars of 4BIG units that were out of service for asbestos removal. Unit 2702 consisted of three coaches of 4CEP 1557 and buffet car S69021 that was formerly in 4BEP 7022. The 4TEPs were short-lived, running for between two and three years only, so to travel in and photograph one was certainly a bonus for us that week!

As if the 4TEPs as units weren't novel enough, books acquired in the years since have revealed that the buffet car involved in this one was unique in itself! Sometime in the mid-1960s, S69021 had been experimentally fitted with pressure ventilation equipment, most of its opening windows being replaced by plain glass. I have always been interested in on-train catering and tried to take photographs of EMU buffet cars on the Southern. There was time on this occasion, as the light faded after a lovely sunny day, for S69021 to have a slide all to itself before it headed off to Bognor or we boarded our train for Havant (whichever came first!) at the end of our first day exploring Area B.

Earlier in the day on 4th June 1984 and another platform 1, this time at Horsham. We are looking at one end of 4EPB 5408, with repeated unit numbers above the cab windows indicating its status as a 'facelifted' unit of Class 415/4. This designation is shown on the blue sticker next to the left hand set of jumper cables. Other data is hand painted in black and the unit carries blue and grey livery.

On the second day of our rover week, 5th June 1984, 4CIG 7322 is seen having arrived at Seaford. Electric services had first reached here in 1935 and this was my first of several visits to the town.

On 5th June 1984, 4VEP 7725 leaves Newhaven Harbour station on its way to Bishopstone and Seaford. The photograph was taken from the footbridge and the tracks leading off to the right served the now disused Newhaven Marine station. Sealink ferries sailed from here to Dieppe, as I remember from a school trip to that French port in 1972. I was in the first year (nowadays referred to as "Year 7") at secondary school on Hayling Island. I can still recall it being a wet day and that the ferry was the "Valencay" – but it was my first taste of any kind of foreign travel!

On 6th June 1984, platform 3 at the spacious Lewes station is occupied by what appears to be an eight car London bound train with 4BIG 7051 at the rear and a 4VEP coupled ahead. I recall that we spent some time in the town, including a visit to the castle, as well as taking several photographs of trains. There were – and still are – the platforms seen here for services connecting London with Eastbourne and Hastings, plus others (out of shot to the left) for services to and from Brighton. A large triangular covered platform area is also out of shot to the left and above it all was a wide enclosed footbridge. On this visit it featured a good second-hand book stall and I still have the one about the television series "Doctor Who" that I bought there that day!

45

46 Looking across to platform 2, we see a down train for Eastbourne led by either a 4BIG or 4CIG – unfortunately I cannot read the number! Waiting passengers, the then current style of black-on-white platform signage and lots of bits of station 'structure' make for a busy scene. While the trains of course now look very different and the signage will have had at least two 'image changes' since I took this picture on 6th June 1984, the essence of it remains the same although – as I am writing these notes 'post-Covid' in early 2023 – I would imagine that the weekday commuter 'peaks' are not what they used to be.

On 6th June 1984, 4CIG 7312 enters platform 6 at Lewes with a service from Brighton to Hastings (headcode 16). Beyond the more distant of the two 'Platform 6' signs can just be seen a double-sided bay platform, which had lost its track by the time of our visit.

47

On 7th June 1984, (before the rain briefly came!), we were at Area B's western extremity at Portsmouth Harbour expecting a working from London of the Venice Simplon-Orient-Express Pullmans. It turned out that it had been cancelled, as a helpful member of BR staff kindly informed us – no doubt because we looked like 'obvious' railway enthusiasts! We managed a couple of photographs of less 'exalted' stock, as represented here by Waterloo-bound 4VEP 7818, before moving on to Chichester and catching up with the rain. At this time, all five platform faces had track – a situation that no longer exists. Waiting in platform 5 is loco 33037, its headcode '89' being that used for trains from Portsmouth to Bristol and Cardiff.

On the penultimate day of our Area B travels, (8th June 1984), facelifted BR-design 4EPB 5315 is seen in platform 4 at Horsham. These later EPB units, which came in two and four car varieties, followed on from construction of the Southern Railway-designed units and were built from the mid-1950s until the last ones were turned out in 1963. The unit carries blue and grey livery and forms a train to Victoria via Mitcham Junction. Readers will note that I use the simpler forms for the names of London terminal stations - e.g., "Waterloo" and "Victoria" - that had been in use for many years when I started travelling (in 1978) and would remain so for some years after that. Only in more recent times has it been thought necessary to prefix all such signage with the word "London".

On 11th May 1985, we visited parts of the Southern Region in slightly more unusual stock, albeit still third rail powered. The "First & Final 501" railtour used two of the three car units that had for many years worked on the North London Line between Broad Street and Richmond and the "DC lines" out of Euston. As the title suggested, this was the only tour ever to feature this stock. Although pictures of the tour train would not fall within the coverage aimed for in this book, I was able to obtain photographs of other trains. One such was S14532S of 4EPB unit 5447, seen at Horsham while the tour had a photo stop there. As the tour ran on a Saturday, we would appear to have just missed "Crunchie Day"!

50

Reference has been made elsewhere in the book to the "crumbling edge of quality" and it certainly seems to be visible in this view taken on 1st June 1985. In contrast to the peeling paintwork on the building, BR-design 2HAP 6063 appears to be presentably clean in its blue and grey livery as it waits in platform 8 at Guildford. We were on our way to an open day at Reading diesel depot, one of several events staged that year for the 150th anniversary of the Great Western Railway. The weather seen here fortunately continued, with the two of us along with probably a few thousand others enjoying a warm and sunny day!

Taken during a day's travels using a Berkshire Day Rover ticket on 26th April 1986, 4REP 3009 is seen at Basingstoke heading a service for Waterloo. What looks like some EPB or HAP stock can be seen on the right and the platform edge white paint would seem to need a 'top-up'!

Also seen at Basingstoke on 26th April 1986 is '3D' DEMU 1310, quite possibly employed on the shuttle service between there and Reading. These three car sets were slightly younger than the 3H variety, dating from the early 1960s. In my opinion, both looked smart in blue and grey livery, especially when freshly outshopped or at least kept clean, but it could be said that as the 1980s progressed, such stock with its many doors and basic (though comfortable) interiors did not help the cause of promoting the railway as a modern means of travel. The final three 3Ds were finally withdrawn in 2004, having achieved forty-two years of service. They only had two of their original coaches by then but had acquired a 4CEP trailer in lieu of the original Trailer Composite. As the ex-CEP coach was of full width and the original 3D vehicles had been built to a narrower profile, this gave an odd appearance with the unit seeming 'fatter' in the middle. I seem to recall the nickname 'Maggots' being offered by some enthusiasts at the time!

53

At Reading on 26th April 1986, we see 4CIG 7417 in one of the two platforms (4a & 4b) then provided for electric services from Waterloo. The separate "Southern" station at Reading had closed in the 1960s and at the time of this image the area was used for car parking. Reading station has in recent years had a large and expensive revamp, with extra platforms and a huge enclosed "footbridge" structure connecting them. It may have more capacity to handle additional services now, but my first impression was that all the new structures seemed to be grey - there was little or no colour. Surely for all the millions of pounds that new or rebuilt stations seem to cost nowadays, could we not have at least some colour to relieve the bland appearance? As I always say about many things, "other opinions are available". In the background can be seen an MCW Metrobus of Reading Transport, still council controlled as I write in early 2023 but one of very few such operators now remaining.

On Sunday 27th April 1986, BR held a 'gala day' to launch the new electric service between London and Hastings via Tonbridge. Reliveried 4CEP units were to replace the narrow bodied DEMUs that had provided motive power on the route since their introduction twenty-nine years earlier. Special fares were available for the day giving unlimited travel between Tonbridge and Hastings but demand soon outstripped supply where the specially printed tickets were concerned, and these rapidly sold out – later arrivals no doubt having to make do with suitably annotated ordinary ones! The weather was unfortunately not at its best, but despite this the trains were busy with perhaps more people supporting the event than might have been expected. Here a crowd waits to board 4CEP 1518 at Tonbridge.

The 4CEP units used on the new electric service had been repainted in a brown, grey and orange livery under the auspices of the London & South East business sector, the introduction of the Network SouthEast identity and livery still being a couple of months away at this time. Due to a perceived resemblance to a certain chocolate and orange flavoured food product, this became widely known as the "Jaffa Cake" livery! On the gala day, an eight car CEP formation led by unit 1528 is seen approaching West St. Leonards station from the Tonbridge direction.

Looking the other way at West St. Leonards station, a train for Tonbridge is led by unit 1522. The weather may appear, in the distance at least, to be trying to brighten up, but all these years later I don't recall that happening! Note that lines of 'bunting' have been put up to give a 'festive' feel to the day.

Unfortunately, insufficient newly reliveried 4CEPs were available for the gala day, so other stock had to be drafted in to help. An example of this is seen at West St. Leonards in the form of 4EPB 5148.

With lots of people visible, (probably mostly enthusiasts!), 4EPB 5142 is seen heading a gala day train at Etchingham. While not presenting an ideal image for a 'new' electric service, trains of EPB stock did at least offer a high seating capacity and did their bit to help shift the crowds.

The most unusual unit seen on the gala day was de-icer 007, seen at Hastings by which time it would appear to be raining. Although the unit had clearly received some depot attention, with silvered buffers and window frames and some other parts painted white, I am not aware that it was supposed to be (nor was it presumably allowed to be) in passenger service. However, it might have acted as some sort of unofficial transport as I do recall at one point seeing a 'side' of Morris Dancers alighting from it – certainly one of the most unusual things I have ever seen at a railway event!

In 1986, boat trains composed of a Class 33/1 diesel loco and 4TC stock were still serving Weymouth Quay using the branch line (often referred to as the 'quay tramway') that left the main line just before Weymouth station. Boat trains passed through the streets at very slow speed, preceded by BR staff on foot. In this view taken on 19th June, 4TC 403 is the rear part of a train heading for the quay station, where passengers boarded ferries to the Channel Islands. As can be clearly seen, road traffic also used the route, and careless or inconsiderate parking could sometimes cause problems for the train. A Ford Escort follows the train, with a Rover behind. An earlier model of Escort is parked to the left, next to what appears to be a blue Renault. An amusing coincidence, in view of the first name of my friend and fellow traveller, can be seen in the sign on the left! On our first visit to Weymouth six years earlier, hauled stock was still being used on the boat trains, with the loco running round at the quay station.

A view taken from the footbridge at Slade Green station on 24th June 1986 shows EMU stock stabled in the sidings next to the depot. The units were probably mostly EPBs, although there might have been a HAP or two in there somewhere! A broadly similar view, with more modern stock, could still be taken today.

On 24th August 1986, a gala event was held at Cannon Street station, closed to normal services as it was a Sunday. Various steam, diesel and electric motive power was on display and a shuttle service to Cannon Street from Charing Cross. Alternating on this were the preserved 2BIL & 4SUB formation featured elsewhere in this book and Class 455 unit 5872 in the new Network SouthEast livery. The latter is seen here at Charing Cross in the company of 4EPB 5035.

A "Southern" unit, but not on the "Southern"! During the time in the mid-1980s that Southern Region stock worked the North London Line, SR-design 2EPB 6328 is seen at North Woolwich station. The old station building behind the train had been converted into a railway museum, with rolling stock housed on track to the left of the picture. The museum has since closed and 'heavy rail' no longer serves the site following extensions to the Docklands Light Railway.

On 4th October 1987, the Southern Electric Group took a 4REP unit to places well away from its usual home 'patch' on the Bournemouth line, visiting among others Tonbridge, Brighton, Folkestone Harbour and Dover Western Docks stations. The tour, with the rather 'corny' name of "The Rep-ar-tie-Sea", was formed of unit 2005 with haulage by loco 33008 between Redhill and Tonbridge. Technical issues with 2005 led to 4CEP 1567 being attached for part of the tour. Wearing an alternative SEG headboard to that seen on the "Electric Phoenix" elsewhere in this book, 2005 is seen at Charing Cross prior to departure. This was before the station had been modernised and redeveloped with the massive building that sits on top of it today. Looking back at this slide now, that edge of the station really looks quite scruffy! I had driven up to Slough the day before to stay with my friend Kevin, who had booked our places on the tour. Unfortunately, by Friday the tickets had not arrived, and we still remember the difficulty we had trying to explain this to the SEG organisers when we got to Charing Cross. "You haven't booked tickets?" "No, we HAVE booked tickets, but they haven't arrived." To our relief, we eventually got them to understand!

65

The "Rep-ar-tie-Sea" tour is seen during a stop at Strood. This unit had originally been 3005 prior to reclassification from Class 430 to 432. The full TOPS unit number in this case would be 432005, but shortened versions were carried according to Southern Region tradition.

Another of my 'arty' shots – or, as Robert and I like to call them, remembering our camera club days, "outbreaks of creativity"! Here is the "Rep-ar-tie-Sea" tour during a photo stop at Deal, where I have made use of the framing effect offered by the footbridge. As if to help with the composition, a Leyland National bus of the East Kent fleet is obligingly crossing the road bridge in the background!

On a sunny 25th July 1987, 4VEP 3116 is in platform 2 at Bournemouth heading an up semi-fast service (headcode 92) to Waterloo. The unit is in Network SouthEast livery with what appears to be the second, darker shade of blue. The livery was initially launched in June of the previous year with a lighter blue. Another unit still in blue and grey livery occupies the short bay platform, number 1.

Another view taken at Bournemouth on 25th July 1987 sees 4TCB unit 2806 leading another buffet car equipped unit into Bournemouth station. This was at the time when the new Class 442 units, using the Mark 3 bodyshell, were being built. The withdrawn 4REPs were to donate their motors for re-use in the new stock, so some temporary formations, sometimes using the ability of Class 33 and 73 locos to work in multiple with Mark 1 EMU stock, existed at this time. The TCBs were essentially a 4TC formation with the trailer first replaced by a 4REP buffet car and for some reason I made a note at the time of the formation of unit 2806! I have a note of it consisting on that day of the driving trailers from 4TC 8013 and the centre two cars from 4REP 2010.

Left: In May 1991 my wife, my in-laws and myself did a three day walk around Chichester harbour. Coach transport was provided from Chichester station to each day's starting point, enabling this unusual use of some handy metalwork (from memory, it was part of the public footbridge) to frame 4CIG 1709 on a train to Victoria via Hove. The picture was taken on 25th May.

Right: In early 1988, I moved out of the family home and bought my first home, a studio flat in Southsea, Portsmouth. Living there for the next five years, Portsmouth & Southsea became my new local station – reached by a ten-to-fifteen-minute walk. Travelling from there one day in February 1991, I was surprised to see 2EPB 6319 on the rear of a train heading for Portsmouth Harbour. Although this was a few years away from final withdrawal of EPB stock, this was the last time that I saw one in our home area.

Left: On 15th April 1995, I was a passenger on the "End of an Era" tour, organised by South Eastern and the Southern Electric Group to mark the end of EPB stock in passenger service. Two units formed the tour train – 5001 which had been restored to green livery and 5176 in blue. Here I am once more indulging in a less than 'standard' pictorial approach during the photo stop at Addiscombe. The distinctive Southern design of windows, with their curved (or "radiused") corners frame an assortment of tour passengers at a station which, following the introduction of Croydon Tramlink, no longer exists.

Right: On 12th January 1991, NSE liveried BR-design 4EPB 5623 was used on the aptly named "EPB to the Sea" tour, which reached Weymouth – a very unusual destination for such stock! Although the tour was run very early in the year the weather was kind, resulting in some very nicely lit slides. Here we see 5623 during the booked stop at Wareham, in NSE livery and complete with Kent Coast logos.

On 12th January 1991, NSE liveried BR-design 4EPB 5623 was used on the aptly named "EPB to the Sea" tour, which reached Weymouth – a very unusual destination for such stock! Although the tour was run very early in the year the weather was kind, resulting in some very nicely lit slides. Here we see 5623 during the booked stop at Wareham, in NSE livery and complete with Kent Coast logos.

Southampton Central on Saturday 14th August 2004, with 'celebrity' 4VEP 3417, (originally new in 1967 as 7717 and restored externally as far as possible to original condition and livery), with sister unit 3812 in South West Trains livery. These two units ran together all day on a Waterloo-Southampton 'shuttle' service, rather grandly billed by SWT as a "Slam-Door Gala"! I worked for Royal Mail at the time, so after finishing work and a quick lunch I travelled by train to Southampton to get some photos. One wonders if the two young ladies, relaxing on the platform on this fine August afternoon, noticed all the people with cameras and wondered what all the fuss was about?!

75

In April 2005, the 'new order' in the form of 'express' five car unit 444039, one of forty-five built by Siemens in Germany, enters Petersfield with a Waterloo service. These had seating in a 2 + 2 layout in standard class, with 2 + 1 in first class. Accompanying the 444s were a hundred and twenty-seven four car Class 450 units with a mostly 3 + 2 seating layout and – rather like the 4VEPs – originally intended for suburban work. Between them, these two classes were to see out the final Mark 1 slam-door stock on the South West Trains network. I had walked along the platform to avoid the crowding of people wanting to board nearer the front. The lady in the leather jacket and rather distinctive red skirt nicely filled what would otherwise have been an empty space in my picture!

On 19th November 2005 train operator Southern and the Southern Electric Group organised the "Sussex Slammer" tour. Another case for me of getting some photographs after work, (railtours do mostly run on Saturdays!), it was fortunate for me that the train was running late. The itinerary had apparently needed to be revised as someone somewhere had omitted to remember that East Grinstead station could not take a twelve-car train! Seen from the road to Burpham as it approached Arundel, the twelve-car train consisted of 4CIGs 1866 and 1805 in Connex livery, 'sandwiching' 4VEP 3514 in the rare Southern colour scheme of two-tone green with white. Several of us had gathered along that road to take pictures and at one point a lady with a child in her car stopped to ask whether a steam train was due. "NO", I told her, "But a special electric one is". Expecting her to instantly lose interest and drive off, I was quite surprised when not only did she park the car, but they both got out to wait with the rest of us and waved as the tour headed for Littlehampton!

Although Mark 1 stock was withdrawn from most of the South West Trains network in 2005, two 4CIG units were shortened to three cars and painted in 'heritage' liveries to work the branch service from Brockenhurst to Lymington Pier. These units were used from May 2005 to May 2010, with 1498 wearing 1960s green livery and 1497 attired in blue and grey. The latter was in charge on the last day, 22nd May 2010. It is seen here crossing the harbour with a service from the Pier station and is about to call at Lymington Town.